This Faber book belongs to

. . . .

For Frank, my brother and fellow Earthling —S. M.

For Katie, Ben, and George —D. L.

For all my humans, especially the ones who recycle! —E.

First published in the US in 2017 by Henry Holt and Company
First published in the UK in 2018 by Faber and Faber Limited
Bloomsbury House, 74–77 Great Russell Street, London WC1B 3DA

Text copyright © 2017 by Stacy McAnulty
Illustrations copyright © 2017 by David Litchfield

The rights of Stacy McAnulty and David Litchfield to be identified as
author and illustrator of this work respectively have been asserted
in accordance with Section 77 of the Copyright, Designs and
Patents Act 1988

Printed in China

A CIP record for this book is available from the British Library

First edition, 2017 / Designed by April Ward

The illustrations for this book were created with pencils, ink, watercolor paints, and digital art tools.

ISBN 978-0-571-34544-1

1 3 5 7 9 10 8 6 4 2

Faber & Faber has published children's books since 1929. Some of our very first publications included *Old Possum's Book of Practical Cats* by T. S. Eliot, starring the now world-famous Macavity, and *The Iron Man* by Ted Hughes. Our catalogue at the time said that: 'it is by reading such books that children learn the difference between the shoddy and the genuine'. We still believe in the power of reading to transform children's lives.

→→ A FABER PICTURE BOOK ←←

Planet AWESOME!

BY Earth (WITH STACY MCANULTY)
ILLUSTRATED BY Earth (AND DAVID LITCHFIELD)

ff

FABER & FABER

Hi! My name is **EARTH.** Some people call me

Gaia

the blue marble

the
WORLd

or the third planet from the sun.

You can call me
PLaNet Awesome.

My family is really, really big.

Neptune

Uranus

Jupiter

Saturn

Mars

Venus

Earth

Mercury

Pluto

The Solar System – say cheese!

I have **seven** siblings in my solar system.

I'm closest to Venus and Mars.

Some used to say I had eight siblings,

but Pluto is more like the family pet.

And then there are my cousins.

My Milky Way family has **BILLIONS** of planets.

Told you. **BIG** family.

My favourite things to do are spinning
(it takes me a whole day to spin round once)

and CIRCLING the SUN.

That takes me an entire year.

My best friend is the moon. We hang out
all the time, even when you can't see her.
The moon takes 27 days, 7 hours, 43 minutes
and 12 seconds to go round me. I've timed her.

I was born **4.54 billion** years ago.

PHOTOS

I don't remember what
it was like to be a baby.
Who does? But I've been
told I was a hot mess.

BABY EARTH

Explosive. Gassy! Very irritable.

Then I started to cool off and things got wet. **Really wet.**

It rained for **thousands** of years.

(I'm not kidding: thousands!)

I was soggy and lonely. A few islands popped up in my oceans, but no plants or animals.

My islands must have been lonely too. They got together and made bigger islands called **continents**.

PANGEA

I remember **UR** and **Nuna** and the ginormous **Pangea**.

Then Pangea split into seven separate continents.

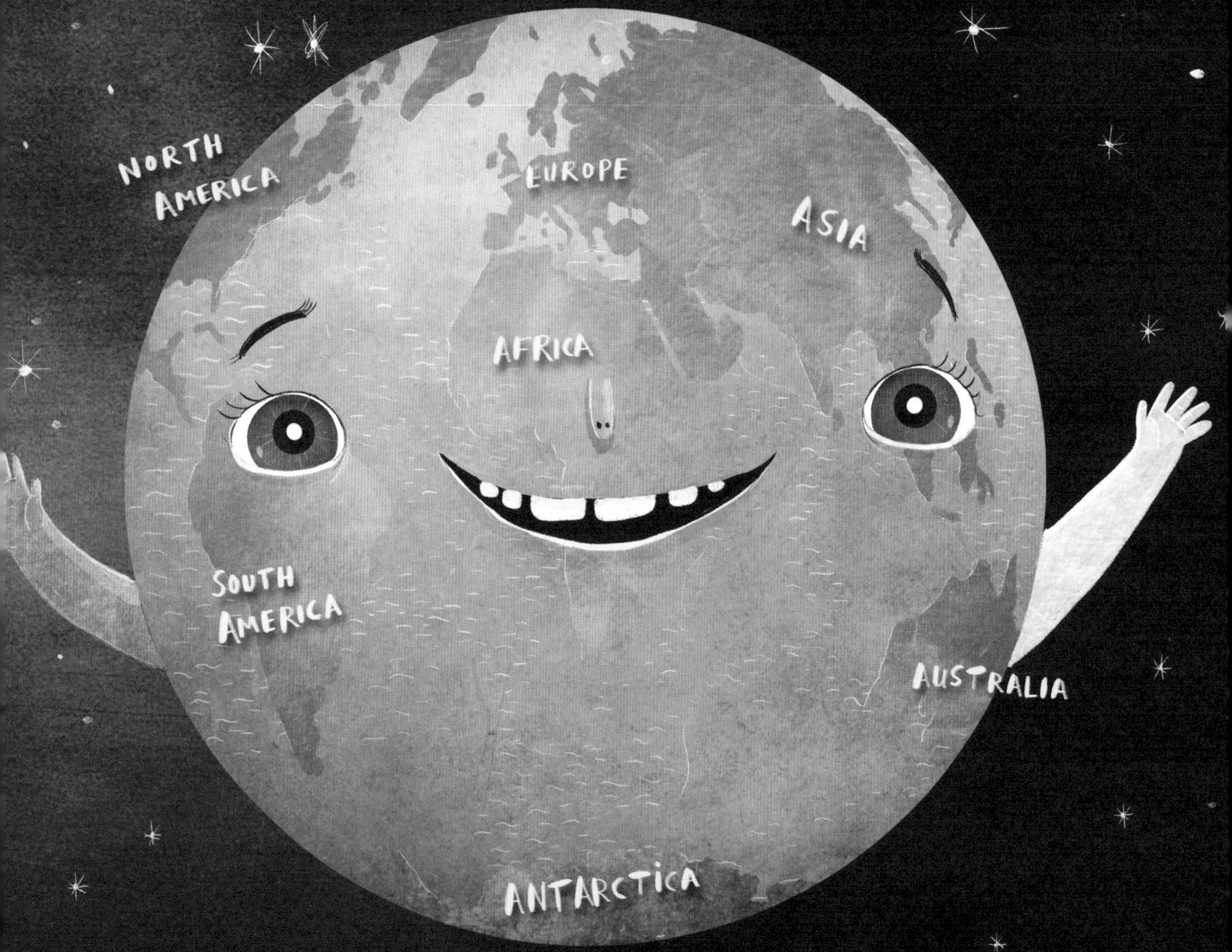

NORTH AMERICA

EUROPE

ASIA

AFRICA

SOUTH AMERICA

AUSTRALIA

ANTARCTICA

Things are always changing.

As I got older, stuff began to grow.
LIFE!

400,000,000
years ago
And then came bugs!

Bzzzzzzz!

For almost half my life, you probably wouldn't even recognise me! (Though I've always been round.)

2,400,000,000
years ago
Air arrived! If anyone had been alive, they could finally take a breath!

470,000,000 years ago
Plants that can live on land appeared.

4,540,000,000
years ago
I arrive!

The time of the
dinosaurs was one
of my favourites.

I mean, everyone loves dinosaurs!
They lived with me for 175 million years.

Until...

ASTEROID!!

It's not always easy being Earth.

Volcanic eruptions.

Ice ages.

Major collisions!

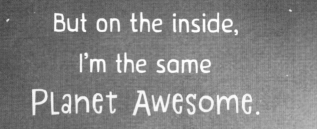

But on the inside,
I'm the same
Planet Awesome.

CRUST

MANTLE

INNER CORE

OUTER CORE

Humans have been great fun.
No other species has ever been
interested in learning about me.

Animals are brilliant too –
they eat and poo
and do a million
incredible things.
They are an
important part
of my amazing
life.

But sometimes humans forget to share and play nicely and clean up after themselves.

Still, I bet you humans will turn out
to do really super things.

MORE FUN FACTS
Continents

Continents are huge chunks of land, sometimes separated by water. Not all geologists agree on the formation and timing of these continents. It would have been easier if there were cameras millions of years ago. But the scientists do agree that Earth's crust is made up of tectonic plates that are still moving. The North American plate and the Eurasian plate are moving apart at a speed of about one inch per year. In a million years, Earth may look quite different.

Location

Earth resides in the Milky Way, along with billions of other planets and suns. (At least 100 billion suns!) Our solar system has only one sun, eight planets, five dwarf planets and about 150 moons. Earth is approximately 93 million miles from the sun, but this varies slightly depending on the time of year.

Life

Earth is a great hostess. She provides air, water, food and shelter. However, every so often she goes through changes that make life difficult. Impossible, even. There have been five major extinctions.

- Ordovician-Silurian extinction (440 million years ago): This had a major impact on marine life. It was probably caused by a severe ice age.

- Late Devonian extinction (360 million years ago): About 75% of all species disappeared.

- Permian extinction (250 million years ago): This has been named "The Great Dying" because more than 90% of Earth's species were destroyed.

- Triassic-Jurassic extinction (200 million years ago): No clear cause for this extinction, but it managed to wipe out about 76% of life on Earth.

- Cretaceous-Tertiary extinction (66 million years ago): Bye-bye, dinosaurs! Theories suggest a deadly combination of volcanic activity, climate change and an asteroid impact on Mexico's Yucatán Peninsula.